The Tiniest Candle

The Tiniest Candle

WRITTEN BY DAMON YOUNGER • ILLUSTRATED BY JOYCE KITCHELL

OAK TREE PUBLICATIONS, INC., LA JOLLA, CALIFORNIA

First Edition
Manufactured in the United States of America
For information write to: Oak Tree
Publications, Inc.
P.O. Box 1012, La Jolla, CA. 92038

Library of Congress Cataloging in Publication Data

Younger, Damon, 1950-
     The tiniest candle.

     Poem.
     SUMMARY: A verse retelling of
the events surrounding the birth of Jesus.
     1.   Jesus Christ — Nativity —
Juvenile poetry. [1.   Jesus Christ —
Nativity — Poetry. 2.   American poetry]
I.   Title.
PZ8.3. Y86Ti   811'.5'4   78-13709

ISBN 0-916392-25-2

FOR TOULA,
RUTH AND FRANK
WITH LOVE

SPECIAL THANKS TO
REVEREND BOB
AND VISSEC

The winter winds whistled and frost nipped the air
As merchants of Bethlehem bargained with care
For the rare herbs and spices and baskets of wheat
Brought in by caravans crowding the street,
And from far and from near, upon every road,
The citizens came to pay taxes they owed.
The crowds parted way when the soldiers rode through,
They had traveled from Rome to collect what was due.

Now on a back corner a candle booth stood,
Where shopkeeper Jalal sold all that he could.
His candles were molded of excellent wax,
And in each was a wick made of very fine flax.
There were thick lights and thin ones, short candles and tall,
And as the day passed, old Jalal sold them all.
All, that is, but one, which was such a small size
That whoever set eyes on it laughed in surprise.

Said one man, "That's a wretched excuse for a light.
Don't ask me to buy it. It won't last a night."
The small taper sighed and it sagged in its stick.
"I'm tiny, it's true, but I have a good wick."
Said the candle, "If you'll only take me along,
I'll shine with a light that is steady and strong."
The man paid no heed to that voice low and meek,
For he never had dreamed that a candle could speak.

When he left, Jalal packed up his things in a sack
Which he slung with a groan to his tired old back.
He went down the alley past fish and fruit stands,
And he looked not at beggars who held out their hands.
He pushed through the crowds to the gates of the town,
Then trudged to the desert as night settled down.
Jalal traveled in silence, but did not go far
To reach his small dwelling beneath the first star.

There he put down his sack and he kindled a blaze.
On wax-coated wood the flames danced 'neath his gaze.
Soon under the table old Jalal caught sight
Of two amber eyes that reflected the light.
A dark shape moved silent around a stool's legs
And crept like a shadow past wax pots and kegs.
"Ah, Tamika!" Jalal smiled down at the cat.
"Be nice and I'll feed you." He gave her a pat.
He yawned while he fixed her some milk mixed with bread,
And he ate some dried dates as he sat on his bed.

When he'd eaten, he picked up the sack he'd let fall,
As the room swayed with shadows that grew short and tall.
He took out the candle and said with a laugh,
"What a pity that you aren't bigger by half.
Tomorrow I'll make sure the fire's quite hot,
And I'll melt down your wax with the rest in the pot."
The fire sparked and popped as it chuckled so sly
At the tiniest candle that no one would buy.
Jalal set it down on a stool near the bed.
He got under the covers and put down his head.
Tamika crawled in to lie at his side,
And soon they both slept as the last ember died.

*T*amika wakened to darkness and chill,
And winds that shook timbers as winter winds will.
Above her the flimsy old roof gave a creak,
And from somewhere close by she could hear a voice speak.
"Please help me escape!" came the soft little cry.
"I know that I'm small, but I don't want to die."
At first the cat trembled and felt a great fear,
Then she saw the small candle shed one waxen tear.

Good Tamika got out of bed and she crept
Close to the stool where the small candle wept.
"Tamika, help me," it begged, "and you'll see
That somewhere there's need for a candle like me."
A sudden wind gusted and blew the door wide.
It rattled the tumbledown walls side to side.
Jalal gave a whimper and turned in his sleep,
But kitty and candle did not make a peep.
The candle then whispered, "Oh please, for my sake,
Take me away now, before he's awake."

So the cat took the candle between gentle jaws,
And she ran out the door on her velvety paws.
As she fled up the road, she felt the wind's bite,
But she never let go of that scared little light.
At the gate of the town was a villainous band
Of beggars and cutthroats. One reached out a hand
And attempted to seize the poor cat by the tail.
Tamika opened her mouth in a wail.

Away the cat fled, for she feared she'd be hurt.
The small candle fell and it rolled in the dirt.
It skittered and bounced in the dust, then it hopped
Straight to the crack 'tween two stones. There it stopped.
The candle looked up from the cleft with a cry.
"Please, Tamika! Help me! I don't want to die!"
But the small candle's plea was unheard and too late.
And the men reeled above it and danced near the gate.
They laughed at the thought of the cat in such fright,
And after a bit they went off through the night.

The east winds grew colder. The candle just shook,
And it waited and waited for someone to look
At the place where it lay on the cobblestone street,
Undisturbed by the passage of hurrying feet.
Now past the great gate in the cold desert night,
The townsmen went home seeking comfort and light.
Not one of them paused when the small candle cried,
''Won't someone look down at the place where I hide?''
At last from close by came a woman's faint plea,
''Please, someone, a light, for it's too dark to see.''

Poor Najima leaned on her stick and bent low
As she hobbled along, dressed in rags head to toe.
The candle peeped out from its crack in the street.
Its waxen heart thrilled as it heard her repeat,
"Oh hear me! Please, hear me! I'm lost in the night!
I'm old and I'm crippled and haven't a light!"
Some wayfarers shoved her. Some laughed in her face.
She moaned and groped on at an unsteady pace.

Then the soldiers called out that the streets must be cleared.
They charged at the crowd as their great stallions reared.
"Oh stop!" cried the woman. "I don't have good sight!
You can't leave me here all alone in the night!"
The soldiers just scorned her and mocked all her pleas,
And they roared with cruel glee when she fell to her knees.
She sobbed as she crouched on the bitter cold stones,
"If I just could get home I could warm my old bones."

The candle then spoke. "I am here on the ground.
Right next to your fingers your light can be found."
She heard the strange voice and she scrabbled at stones
And searched like an old dog just hungry for bones.
Her work-roughened fingers felt deep in each crack,
As winds snatched at the poor rags that covered her back.
Three drunken men reeled down the street shouting names.
"Old woman!" they called, as they danced out their games.
They pranced wild about her and sang a mad song,
And spilled the red wine on their shadows so long.

Her hand grasped the candle. She lifted it high
Toward the torches the drunken men held to the sky.
The wick flamed to life and the old woman turned
And crept off through the night while the small candle burned.
It shed its glow on her as homeward she went.
When she reached her own door it was scarcely half spent.
She entered her house and went straight to her bed,
And she lit the large candle which stood at its head.

She blew out the small flame and stared at the smoke
That curled up from the wick. "I thought the thing spoke,"
Said the woman. "I thought it called out from the dirt,
Like a guardian spirit, to keep me from hurt.
My head's all areeling. My brain must be weak,
To think that a wretched wax candle could speak."
But the old woman trembled. She'd had a great fright.
She opened her door and she tossed out the light.
It flew through the air and it bounced on the earth.
Then it lay in the darkness — a thing of no worth!

rascal named Salim came striding downhill.
He'd stolen a wineskin and drunken his fill.
He'd fallen asleep while the sun was still high,
But he'd wakened to thirst and a cloudy night sky.
Through the darkness he saw where the small candle lay.
He snatched it up quickly and went on his way.
"Some poor soul has lost this," he said, "and I think
I'll go straight to the tavern and trade it for drink."

He marched to the tavern and boldly walked in.
He strutted about with his sly, toothless grin,
And he offered the candle in trade for a drink.
The innkeeper chuckled and winked a broad wink.
"That thing in your hand," said the keeper so smug,
"Is not worth the foam that spills out of a mug."
The other men howled and the scoundrel spun round.
Then he ran out and flung the wax light to the ground.

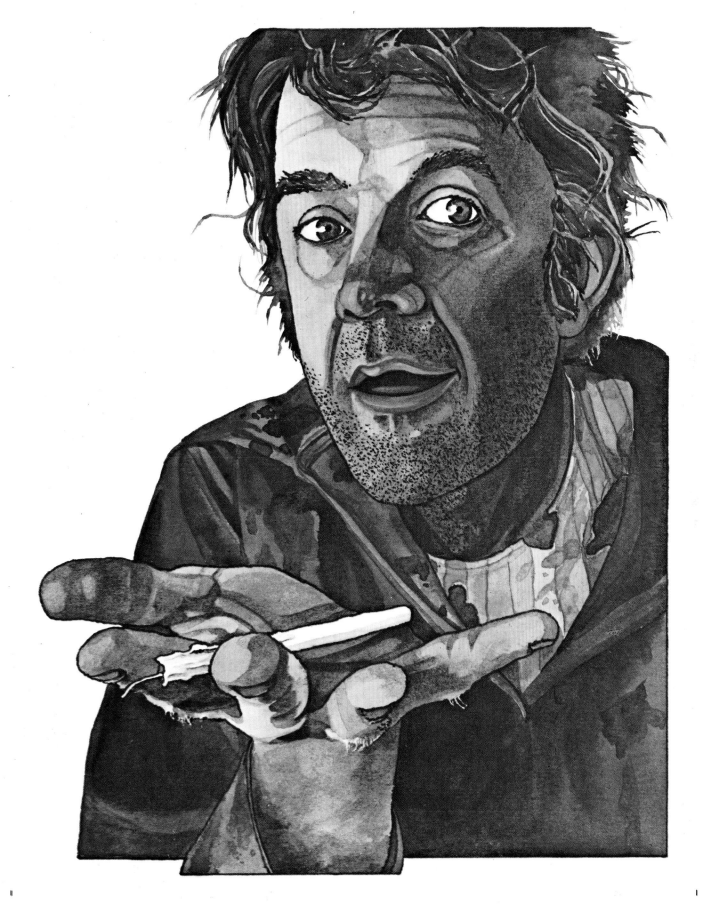

The lost candle sobbed as it said, "I'm too small.
I'm no good to anyone – no good at all!"
Just then a few raindrops came spattering down.
They turned to a torrent that swept o'er the town.
Soon a raging stream poured down the inky black lane.
It caught up the candle, which cried out in vain.
The morsel of wax was caught fast in its grip,
And was washed to and fro like a tiny lost ship.

The water ran deeper and onward it flowed
Into the ditches that bordered the road.
The candle spun round as it bounced over crags,
And dipped into whirlpools around some tree shags.
Past all of the houses it bobbed and it reeled,
Till it floated to ground in a large open field.
There the small candle lay drenched and forlorn
While the rain ceased as quickly as it had been born.

Soft through the night that was suddenly still
Came the bleating of sheep from the flock on the hill.
Close to the field where the small candle lay,
There was a rude stable, sweet-smelling of hay.
A lowing sound floated on chilling night air
From the gentle-eyed cattle that were quartered there.
Next to the stable there stood a large inn
Where the voices of travelers made a great din.
At the inn door a donkey stood stamping the earth.
On his back was a woman who soon would give birth.
Her husband, good Joseph, a man who loved God,
Looked up at his young wife and saw her head nod.
They'd come but to render to Caesar his due,
And found the town filled with both Roman and Jew.

They'd tried every hostel they'd passed on their way,
But each one was full, so they'd no place to stay.
"We must trust in the Lord, for He's helped us before,"
The man said as he stepped up and knocked on the door.
He heard the latch lifted. The door opened wide.
The innkeeper stood there. "You can't come inside.
I'm sorry, good sir, but we're full. There's no room."
The man let the door slam with an echoing boom.
Poor Joseph looked back and he saw Mary's face.
Would her dear child be born in this bare, windswept place?
"Innkeeper! Listen!" he shouted in fright.
"My wife will give birth e'er the end of the night!"
The door rattled open. The innkeeper stout
Pointed back to the stable. "Stay there!" he called out.

The door closed again as the man strained to see
The shadowy place where their shelter would be.
He found the rude shed where beasts snorted with fear.
He calmed them and then turned to Mary so dear.
He carried her in to a place near a stall,
And he kissed her brow gently, then stood up quite tall.
"We must have some light," he said, starting to look
In each corner and cranny, each crack and each nook.
He said, "Lord, in your wisdom you rule night and day.
Please send us a light. This is all that I pray."
Then he walked to the fields and he turned weary eyes
To the clouds that still churned in the black winter skies.
He waited a moment, then looked down and saw,
At his feet in the mud, a small thing like a straw.
He bent to the earth and he picked up the stick.
Then he brushed off the mud and discovered a wick.

Then Mary called out that the child's birth was near.
Joseph saw on the hilltop a bright light appear.
There were fine flaming torches some shepherds had made,
So they tended their sheep in the glow, unafraid.
Joseph ran toward the shepherds. Each man raised his staff.
Joseph called, "I need light!" and he heard the men laugh.
"We'll not spare a torch! No, not for ten kings!
We need all the light for the safety it brings."
Joseph smiled round at the poor ragged band.
"Can I light this?" he asked, and he held out his hand.
"What a miserable candle!" one shepherd exclaimed.
But Joseph reached out to the torches that flamed.
The shepherds who watched shook their heads and they sighed.
Flames licked the damp wick, then they sputtered and died.

"That candle's too small," said one man, "and it's wet!"
But the candle did light with the dimmest flame yet.
Joseph thanked the men kindly and hastened away
To the place down the hill where his sweet Mary lay.
Just then to the town in a caravan grand
Rode three mighty kings who had crossed the bleak land.
From Sheba and Seba and Tarshish, with gold
And perfumes so rare, rode these kings wise and bold.
Their servants called, "Hearken! Rich presents we bring,
To gladden the heart of the newly born king."
One slave hailed the shepherds. He showed them a ring.
"This is yours if you have any word of the king."

The shepherds bowed down and their voices were meek.
"We know only Herod. Which king do you seek?"
Spoke the slave, "A new king who will rule man and beast.
Full long we have followed his star from the east."
The men shook their heads. "We've met no one this night
Except a poor man who was asking for light."
"I see," said the slave, "and where did the man go?"
They all pointed down to the stable below.
The slave gave them jewels and he hurried away
To tell the wise kings what the shepherds did say.

At first the poor shepherds were stunned at the gift.
Then they looked to the sky and they saw the clouds lift.
A blue-flaming star blazed its way through the veil,
And made other lights in the heavens look pale.
The shepherds stared up and they trembled with fear.
Then they dropped to their knees as the new star came near.
They heard a strange voice that was not of this earth.
"Fear not!" spoke the voice. "'Tis the night of His birth!"
A marvelous echoing filled the whole sky,
As choirs of angels sang, "Praise God on high!"

Over the stable the bright star stood still.
The shepherds, all wondering, came down from the hill.
Then outside the stable there gathered a crowd.
There were shepherds and kings. There were angels who bowed.
Good Joseph appeared. "Come within and behold.
It has all come to pass as the prophets foretold."
In silence they entered. They bowed down to praise,
And Mary smiled sweet in the candle's dim rays.
The newborn child Jesus lay warm on her breast,
And His tiny hand stretched toward the candle so blest.

The flame grew and sparkled, then grew larger still.
It filled the whole stable. Its glow lit the hill.
Soon every deep valley, each mountain above,
Felt the warmth of that flame that burned with pure love.
And each man beheld on that dark winter night
That the tiniest candle could make a great light.

And so ends the story of that little light
Which shone on the birth of the Christ child that night.
Now you know that your gift, whether mighty or small,
May well be the light that will brighten us all.